WELCOME HOME™

Kaffe Fassett

WELCOME HOME™
Kaffe Fassett

Edited by Marjon Schaefer

President: Jeramy Lanigan Landauer
Vice President: Becky Johnston
Editor in Chief: Marjon Schaefer
Managing Editor: Marlene Hemberger Heuertz
Graphic Designer: David Jordan
Contributing Editor: Candace Ord Manroe
Associate Editor: Sarah Reid
Photography: Debbie Patterson; Craig Anderson Photography

Published by Martingale & Company
PO Box 118, Bothell, WA 98041-0118 USA

An Imprint of Martingale & Company

This book is printed on acid-free paper.
Printed in Hong Kong 10 9 8 7 6 5 4 3 2 1

Library of Congress Cataloging-in-Publication Data
Kaffe Fassett, 1937-
Welcome Home / Kaffe Fassett ; edited by Marjon Schaefer
p.   cm.
Includes index.
ISBN 1-56477-278-0
1. Textile crafts. 2. House furnishings. 3. Interior decoration.
I. Schaefer, Marjon II. Welcome Home / Kaffe Fassett
TT699.F373 1999
746.9—dc21   99-25648
CIP

Contents

Making a House a Home

8

Changing Rooms 10

Function First 14

Creative Containment 20

Softening the Scene

44

Pattern and Color 46

Quilts, Pillows, and Rugs 54

Setting the Stage

26

Different Strokes 28

Finishing with Fabrics 32

Papers Plus...Collage 34

Cool Surfacing with Tile 38

Making the Most of Mosaic 42

Creating the Mood

Inspiring Collections 62

Accents and Accessories 68

60

74

Museum Tour

Projects and Creativity

Quilts and Instructions 86

Pillows and Instructions 106

Rag Rugs and Instructions 108

Mosaics and Instructions 116

84

Acknowledgments 126

Where to Buy Supplies 127

Foreword

It's always a strange and difficult task to sum up one's life in the form of a book. I think you can see from these shots of my house and studio that I create in a very instinctive and organic fashion. A big part of my inspiration comes from the magical world of past decorative arts. This accounts for the drawers of old textiles, chests of china pots, shelves of marquetry and tin boxes, collections of fans and beaded bags, and masses of colourful books on the subject. The natural world, too, feeds me many ideas, só butterflies, rocks, shells, and dried flowers fill many a corner in my home.

I'm always trying different decorating schemes to see how they look, so a chaos of textures results as several different trails can occur in each room. The main thing that keeps me sane in all this creative madness is that ideas emerge that result in paintings, textile prints, needlepoint, patchwork, and knits. Very often a good inspiration arrives from a pile of rags or yarn of pleasing colors. Since I find this overcrowded world so versatile for my designing, I keep adding to it rather than clearing away and trying to create simple, restful spaces.

Sometimes people are left a bit bewildered by the amount of mediums I work in. To date I've written nine books—about needlepoint, knitting, patchwork, design, and mosaics—and all of them dealt with identical elements. Color and pattern are my obsessions, and playing with them in different mediums leads to a stimulating life.

If you have used my fabrics, needlepoint, knitting, mosaic, or patchwork ideas, perhaps you have some curiosity about the origin of these. I hope you enjoy perusing this book, wandering around and taking in the crowded world where they were born.

Kaffe Fassett

"Since I find this overcrowded world so versatile for my designing, I keep adding to it rather than clearing away and trying to create simple, restful spaces."

Introduction

Working with Kaffe Fassett and his studio is always a great joy for me. In 1995, Kaffe's lecture here at the Minneapolis Institute of Arts was quite well received. So, a year later when I was asked by Dr. Evan Maurer, the Museum's director, to develop an exhibition suitable for the opening of our new First Bank gallery, I immediately thought of Kaffe Fassett. His work would have broad appeal and excite an audience with little or no background information about textiles, as well as satisfy the more traditional museum visitor who frequently has considerable knowledge about the subject.

The instantaneous pleasure derived from seeing something created by this artist is an emotional lift experienced by almost everyone who comes in contact with his work. For those with training in the arts, particularly in the design and textile fields, more than just emotions become engaged. From November of 1997 to mid-February of 1998, when Kaffe Fassett's work was on view here at the Museum, I would frequently visit the exhibition and be intellectually stimulated and inspired by the subtle use of color and line, and the integrated artistic sensibility in each piece.

This book should prove a double joy for the reader. At first glance, enjoy the sheer pleasure of visual delight. Look again, but more carefully, to discover, understand, and appreciate the many levels of artistic expertise incorporated into Kaffe Fassett's work. Would that all learning could be made such a positive experience!

Lotus Stack
Curator, Textiles Department
Minneapolis Institute of Arts

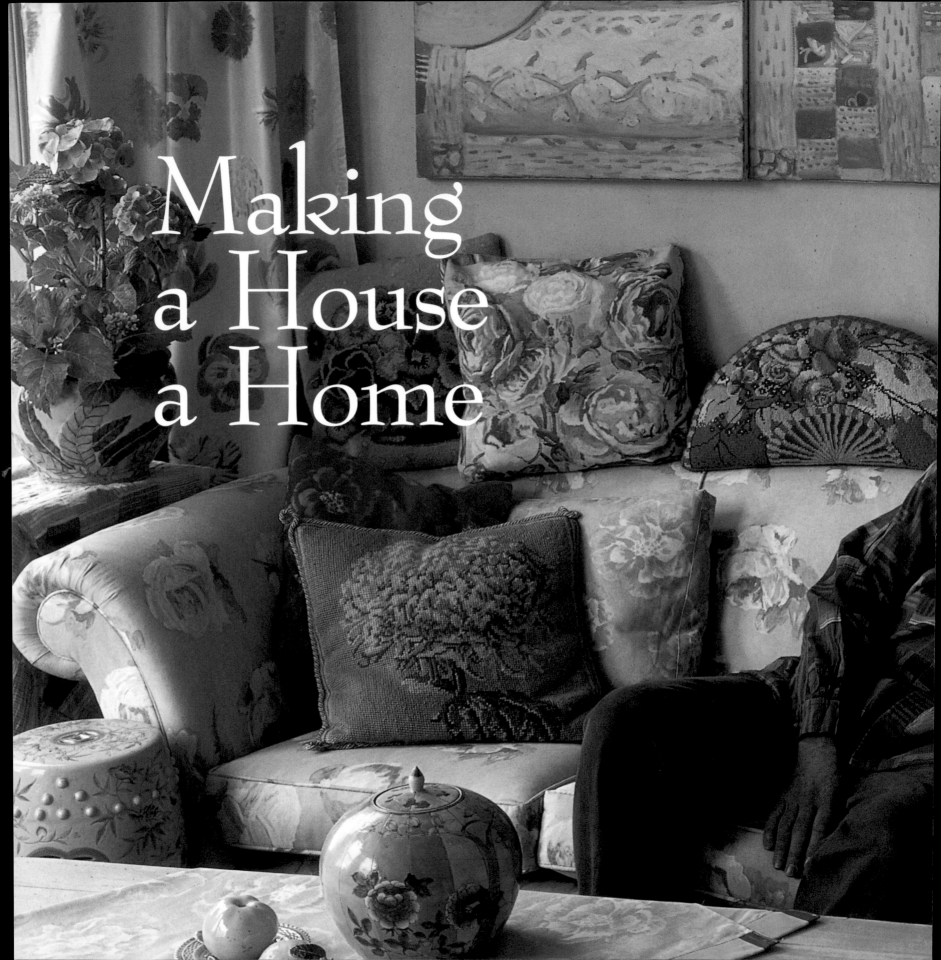

Making a House a Home

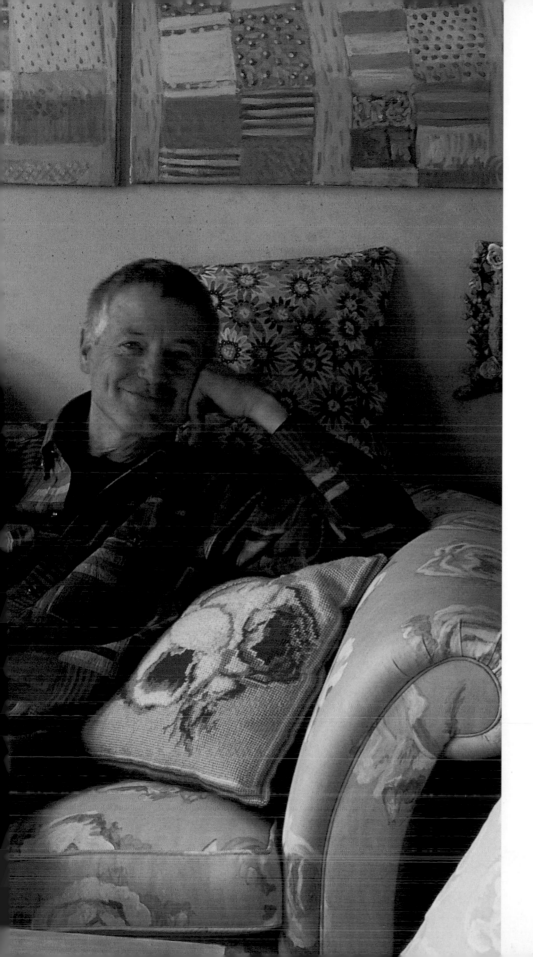

If the distinguishing difference between a house and a home lies in the details, the three-story Edwardian residence of artist Kaffe Fassett is unequivocably a home. Details abound upon each wall, window, shelf, and floor; in every corner and cupboard; and upon each furnishing and fabric of his London domicile. As one-of-a-kind imprints of the homeowner, all of the details stand as a single, unanimous testament: This is clearly, proudly, Kaffe's home. Not even a mirror could prove more telling.

Changing Rooms

Born in San Francisco in 1937, Kaffe first moved to London to paint at age 19, relinquishing a scholarship to the Museum of Fine Art School in Boston after only a 3-month stint. He returned to London, this time to reside permanently, in 1964.

"I came to Britain because I liked the sense of humor and clarity of thought," Kaffe explains. "Soon I fell in love with the soft light, love of gardens, and lack of hype. This allowed me to develop my craft without someone commercializing it before it was fully formed."

That craft—Kaffe's modest appraisal of what is surely art—is fully formed today, even by his own exacting standards. It extends beyond painting, his constant love, to include the textile arts of needlepoint, quilting, and fabric design, for which he has become world-renowned.

But how does all that relate to making a house a home? Very simply. Kaffe uses each of these mediums to personalize his house. In fact, his entire home is something of a studio—or at least a test canvas—where his latest ideas and innovations are experimentally displayed in ever-changing combinations.

Left: An original Kaffe Fassett triptych distinguishes the living room wall in Kaffe's London home. The inset photo shows the same area in one of its altered stages.

Preceding Page: The yellow-background chintz curtains "Fassett's Flowers" and sofa fabric "Fresco Rose" are part of Kaffe's Rosamundi line for Designers Guild.

Above: Two very different looks of the same fireplace wall in the living room attest to the changeability of a room when color and pattern choices are made not just for furniture and accessories but walls as well.

Left: Kaffe gathered shards during walks across Hampstead Heath, a London park area, to fashion his first mosaic—his living room fireplace. He designed and painted the tiles inset into the mosaic, and also made the mosaic pot on the hearth.

11

Changing Rooms

Left: In Kaffe's paint studio, one of the walls features a collage he designed for one of his many books. At that time the room was used as a bedroom, below, but as his needs change so do the rooms.

"The house is like a constantly changing set," Kaffe says. "As I need a background for a new chair, a set of cushions, or a theme for a chapter in one of my books (he has written several on his textile arts), I will paint or paper the walls, or cover them with fabric, lay in new carpets, arrange needlepoint chairs or crockery or whatever, to achieve a look." Some rooms, remain a bit more constant than others. "The leaf dining room, and rose-painted living room—these give the house a certain sense of continuity," he explains.

Kaffe constantly conceives new designs, which manifest themselves in products from mosaic kits to quilt designs, needlepoint projects to licensed fabric lines, on to all sorts of household items from ceramic teapots to placemats, and his rooms reflect the full sweep of his creativity. Color schemes change; motifs change; textures change; rooms change. But Kaffe's design style remains intact, despite the diversity: "You could call my style 'thoughtful kitsch' or 'embarrassment of riches' or 'the more the merrier.'" Lavishly layered in pattern on pattern, in a palette that seems to span the spectrum, Kaffe's style is always rich.

Even one of the downstairs rooms is likely to undergo a disarming change of appearance, depending on the style, colors, and theme Kaffe's work is taking at the moment. What once was a bedroom, above, is now the mosaic studio, left. The vibrant patchwork wallpaper collage is effective, inspiring, and equally at home in either setting.

Function First

Just because Kaffe's rooms are so visually rich doesn't mean they exist for aesthetics only. They first and foremost must be hard-working. Nothing illustrates this better than the space known as the "Nerve Center"—the main office desk situated between the painting studio and the fiber studio, on the third floor.

Brandon Mably, Kaffe's studio manager and fellow designer, works here. Although the space clearly is all about work, it's also about fun—and, always, about good design.

"A room should function, but be amusing and lively to the eye at the same time."

Left: An eccentric collection of finds from Kaffe's worldwide travels includes treasured miniature vegetable teapots from Thailand, plus a humorous photograph of Kaffe and Brandon with Sister Scolastica from Germany, which appeared on their '98 Christmas card.

Opposite: Brandon Mably—studio manager and fellow designer—takes care of business at the "Nerve Center."

Function First

Kaffe not only insists that his rooms be functional, but he also demands that each furnishing pull its weight, accomplishing something besides merely occupying space. Kaffe is an avid reader, who constantly draws from his impressive collection of books for ideas and design inspiration. To accommodate the overflow of volumes, he made efficient use of a hallway wall by outfitting it with shelves.

Not surprisingly, many of Kaffe's furniture choices are case goods—cupboards, armoires, shelving units— with intrinsic storage capacity. Instead of dressing a hallway with a decorative console table, which has limited function, a tall cupboard is Kaffe's preference.

Above: French and English kitchenware atop a book shelf project the strong graphic design so prized by Kaffe.

Left: An unstudied air pervades Kaffe's hallway library. Books appear to be read and used, not just purchased and forgotten. Even the orderliness of a library isn't beyond a touch of humor in Kaffe's design. Kaffe's collection of slides, chronicling his many travels, add shape, form, and color contrast to the vertical volumes.

Not only does the cupboard, left, offer closed-drawer storage, it also has open shelving for an artistic presentation of Kaffe's favorite collections. Kaffe's collections span a vast range, reflecting his diverse interests. "Mostly strength and romance in design attracts me," he says. Those qualities are especially apparent in blue-and-white pottery (a mix of English and Oriental), which is featured in compelling still-life vignettes throughout the house.

Above: Kaffe found this pair of Victorian portrait vases in an antiques shop near Washington, D.C.
Left: A massive pine cupboard with several fabulous collections of pottery adds intense drama to the first-floor hallway.

Function First

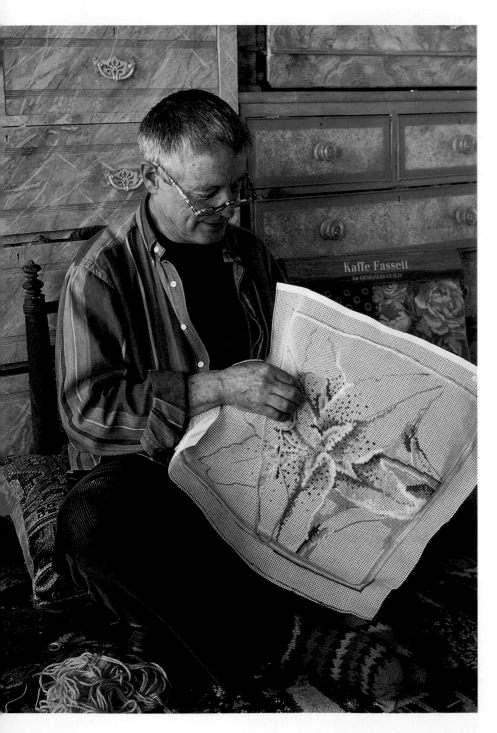

Kaffe's attention to color,

composition, and collectibles

thrives as well in his

work studios as it does in

his living spaces.

Kaffe's first needlepoint design was commissioned by Pamela Lady Harlech for Lord Harlech. Since then, his commissions have included department stores, cruise liners, Elizabethan houses, American theaters, and even a tapestry weaving company in Scotland. Since 1978, he has been the leading needlepoint designer for Ehrman Tapestries of London. Currently at work on a new flower series, Kaffe finds all his materials close at hand. In his at-home fiber studio, supplies are conveniently stored in a succession of tall, colorful, faux-finished chests along one wall and in a bevy of baskets overflowing with richly colored yarns along the opposite wall.

Left: Soft afternoon light filters into the third-floor studio window where Kaffe needlepoints a flowered pillow design.

Those walls in the fiber studio that aren't covered by the tall, whimsically finished storage chests are still hard-working, both visually and functionally. Kaffe's paintings are dotted across one wall, teaming up with a work-in-progress quilt and its different colorways. The combination of permanent and transitory seems exactly what's needed for an eye-pleasing arrangement.

Left: The Tumbling Blocks quilt fragments led to a complete quilt. Inspiration for the new quilt? An old one.

Creative Containment

One of the secrets to Kaffe's successful storage of objects out in the open is to keep the grouping free-flowing, or at least to suggest as much. His is rather the opposite of a rigid, tightly controlled look: books aren't sectioned off according to height, but are allowed to stand together in a looser fashion, directing the eye up and down in joyful, swinging rhythm. The end result is not only greater visual interest, but an appearance of greater authenticity, too. Kaffe's groupings maintain an innocence which stands in direct opposition to a "decorated" look.

More than any other room in the home, the kitchen typically poses the biggest storage challenge (unless the owner happens to be a textiles artist—then storage is an issue throughout). Kaffe solves the problem visually, as one might expect. Instead of exclusive behind-closed-doors storage, he opts for front-and-center displays as well. Decorative plates march along the wall

at near-ceiling height; bowls, teapots, and planters mingle on a top shelf; and a bright assembly of mismatched cups fills the shelf below—some cups standing neatly side-by-side, others hanging from old-fashioned cup hooks. An assortment of exotic teas and condiments that are either prettily packaged or same-shaped to form an eye-pleasing combination sits on the lowest shelf.

Right: Kaffe's home is not without sets of matching china, but his painter's eye finds beauty in the mismatched. "A room should function, but be amusing and lively to the eye at the same time," he says.

Creative Containment

What in less skilled hands might amount to clutter manages to be a decorative tableau. In Kaffe's living room, the vibrant hues of seemingly hundreds of different patterned textiles peek out from cupboard drawers and cubby holes and spill over chairs and onto the floor. But instead of appearing unruly, the medley looks so good that it's clear it must be intentional.

Kaffe reinforces that intentional look by assembling a collection of ceramics in the same space, repeating the full-gamut color palette. A flea-market chair, cleaned, painted, and featuring his own one-of-a-kind needlepoint design, picks up the air of exuberance, pulled in close to the hodgepodge of textiles.

Right: Bursting at the seams with colorfully patterned textiles, a living room storage cabinet becomes a focal point when topped with a crown of ornate pottery and china.

Ever mindful of storage needs, Kaffe even put the awkward area beneath the staircase to utilitarian function, outfitting it with a storage cabinet, which he then integrated into a mural design. Of course, besides functionality, the area provides a surface for displaying art.

"Mostly strength and romance in design attracts me."

Left: Kaffe chose to cleverly cover the once dark staircase niche in fool-the-eye fashion with original floral paintings on canvas by London needlepoint artist Jill Gordon.

Making a House a Home   Creative Containment

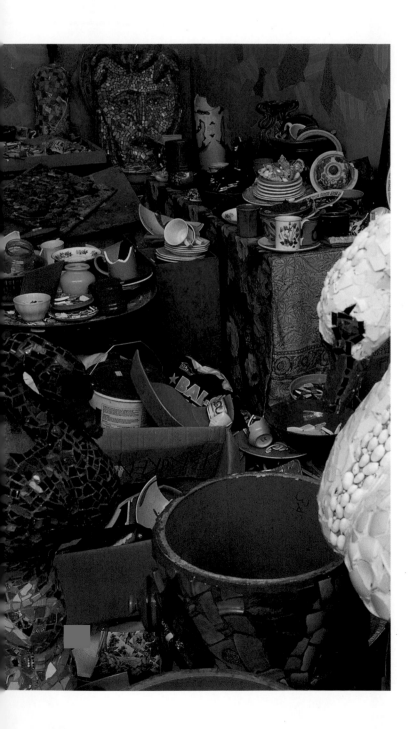

But back to the question, how does Kaffe make his house a home? Most importantly, he uses it to its fullest. Every nook, cranny, and surface area has a purpose and a function. An area such as the mosaic room tends to get dusty, dirty, and messy at the snap of the tile cutting tool, so supplies are stored in pots, bulging boxes, and colorful stacks. In other rooms, storage comes in countless ways. In the fiber studio, Kaffe stacked found dressers on top of each other to create a wall of storage drawers, taking the opportunity to enhance the surfaces with a faux-marble treatment done by a friend from Holland. Baskets and bowls from all over the world overflow with balls and hanks of Rowan yarn in every texture, thickness, and color. Even a chair seat is called upon to hold a pile of folded fabrics—a display seemingly casual and spontaneous, but one that clearly articulates Kaffe's keen eye for color, pattern, and texture.

"I am basically a painter

and have shows every few

years," says Kaffe.

"I squeeze it in with

everything else, between

promo travels, designing

textiles and mosaics, and

writing books."

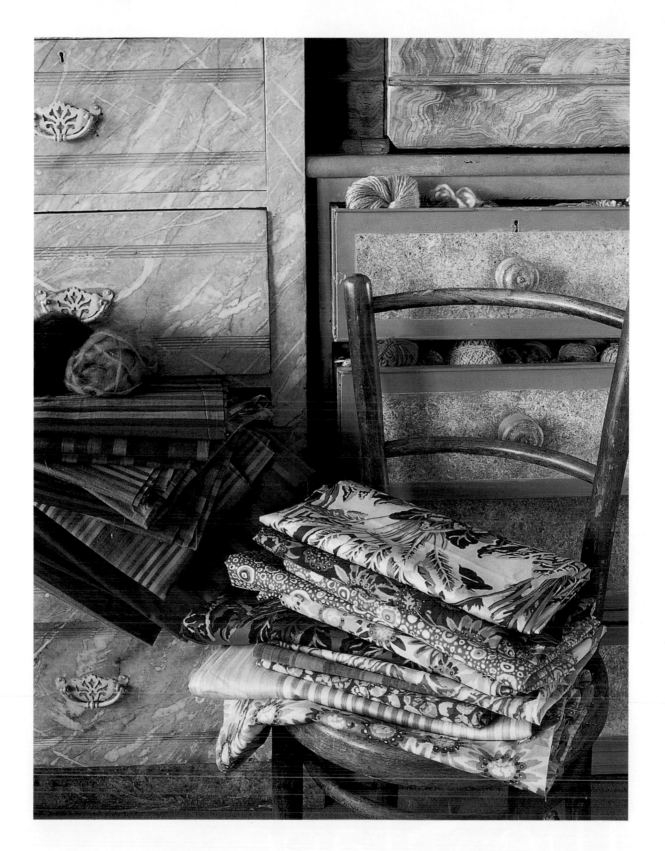

Opposite: Supplies for mosaic work are stored in easy-to-find piles and boxes.

Right: Drawers filled with the fibers of Kaffe's trade—brightly patterned fabrics he's designed and luxurious yarns—have a decorative function as well. Storage need not be boring.

Setting
the Stage

To Kaffe, every surface of his home is an invitation to decorate. Each wall, counter, cupboard—even the fireplace—is a blank canvas awaiting whatever pattern and palette he might favor at the moment. The specific decorative looks will change, but one thing remains constant: Nothing goes unadorned—or even colored only in solids (much too tame an approach for Kaffe's taste). Pattern is a must, whether it's an intermittently applied floral design scattered across a wall, or the ragged-edge geometry of odd-shaped mosaic tiles.

Different Strokes
Strokes

As the main public area of his home, Kaffe's living room is an arena for showcasing his latest creative efforts. But it's also a place for harnessing his creative energies. His current wall decoration is a case in point. The handpainted roses on the living room's pale, antique-yellow walls inspired "The Rosamundi Rose" furnishing fabric collection Kaffe designed for Tricia Guild's Designers Guild.

The wall treatment shows Kaffe's sensitivity to site—the mellow patina of the buttery paint suggests a vintage appropriate for an Edwardian building. (Plus, yellow is the quintessential English color—and an easy, cheery one to live with, day to day.) Over the yellow, Kaffe handpainted big, splashy old-fashioned roses, setting a theme to be repeated on rugs and furnishings.

Left: Kaffe even continued his handpainted floral pattern onto the window, as a bright garland cascading down from the window top.

"Perhaps I am heading toward a slightly simpler arrangement with softer colors. I don't really have a future mapped out. Old worlds and the texture of aging inspire me."

Left: Proof of Kaffe's bold mastery of color is in his juxtaposition of the vibrant crimson chair against the pale yellow walls. The rose pattern repeats on both the needlepoint-covered chair and on the wall—a violation of Decorating 101 that Kaffe pulls off with success.

Different Strokes

One of Kaffe's most ingenious wall
treatments decorates the angled cubby
beneath a staircase. Instead of dismissing
this as "dead space," as many home
owners would, Kaffe saw an opportunity
for artistry. And, this time, not even his
own. Cleverly, he adapted the floral
still-life paintings on canvas of talented
English needlepoint artist Jill Gordon to
serve as a form of wall paneling. He sized
and cut picture mouldings to fit around
the paintings, with the end result being a
sort of trompe l'oeil mural: the bouquets
appear to be murals painted directly onto
the wall. But Kaffe isn't content with only
displaying the work of a fellow artist. In
his kitchen, he wields the brushes and
paints the cabinets himself, decorating the
doors with the blue-and-white pottery
patterns he admires so much as a collector.

*Right: When mounted
to the walls with picture
moulding, Jill Gordon's
masterful artwork looks
convincingly mural-like.*

Above and right: Kaffe often tells his students to "just play with the colors." Putting his inspiring words into practice, he painted the kitchen cabinets while the production crew for this book was on location: On Day 1, we took a photograph of the plain cabinet doors, right. On Day 3 Kaffe started putting color into the outlines he had drawn, far right. On Day 5 the cabinet doors were done, above.

Finishing with Fabrics

Fabrics

Creative paint applications are only one way to dress a wall. Kaffe is equally comfortable cloaking his walls in fabrics—especially fabrics he has designed. And because all of Kaffe's designs begin as paintings, his finished fabrics bear a distinct painterly quality that distinguishes them from other prints. Kaffe's fondness for floral motifs, for stylized but recognizable renderings of his subjects, and for audacious mixes of color, are all evident in his fabrics.

Always apparent is Kaffe's signature way with color— never uniform or singular, but a masterly blend of shades, tones, and seemingly incompatible hues, for a palette of deep complexity.

Left: Kaffe celebrates color, pattern, and floral motifs throughout his home, from his floral rag rug (his own design) to his needlepointed chair (again, a Kaffe design).

Opposite: Colors on this room's wallfabric are repeated on the chair and in accessories for lively results.

33

Papers Plus... Collage

Color is the key to Kaffe's successful blending of diverse materials and motifs. No matter how many colors he combines within a single design or within a single space, Kaffe makes the mix work. One way is by keeping all the colors close in value, so that none pops out as stronger than the others. When that occurs, Kaffe can then contradict his own formula for success, adding a small decorative accessory that features colors of a different value—for example, the brightly dressed doll in a soft, pastel setting on the staircase landing.

Left: A still-life painting illustrates Kaffe's design principle concerning color: Keep all values close, for can't-miss visual harmony. The wallpaper, designed by Kaffe, helps set the stage.

Above: The striped wallpaper in the paint studio is the perfect counterpart to an elaborately patterned chair.

Opposite: Flavia, a doll made by Kaffe, is a colorful standout in this pastel setting, which features Kaffe's wallpaper as a backdrop. The repetition of what Kaffe terms "high blue" is his explanation for the success of the color mix.

Papers Plus...Collage

If Kaffe subscribes to any design rule, it's "no rules, please"—or at least that's the message communicated by the astonishing decorative surfaces in his home. Who ever said a single wall must be covered in a single material, be it paint, wallpaper, or fabric? Certainly not Kaffe. Proof is his "scrap" wall—a layer upon layer collection of wallpapers, fabrics, and original color sketches. And if that's not enough, he even tops the montage with a china-painted plate—a sure sign of this artist's confidence in his skills at mixing mediums. Kaffe's home features other scrap collages. Most notable is a four-panel folding screen in the dining room that he made using magazine cut-outs, wallpapers, and other materials that caught his eye.

Above: A sense of artistic imagination thrives on this scrap wall designed by Kaffe. Pinned onto wallpaper remnants is the original color sketch he made for his "The Rosamundi Rose" furnishing fabric for Designers Guild.

Left: Flowered postcards all pieced together create yet another version of wallpaper.

Opposite: A robust autumn palette prevails in the dining room, which features decorative items designed by Kaffe, including a folding collage screen and a brilliant garden-themed quilt.

37

Tile

Cool Surfacing with Tile

Pattern takes many forms, and Kaffe is fascinated with exploring the possibilities presented by tiles. Mosaics composed of irregularly shaped shards achieve the most variety, but even surfaces covered in uniformly sized square tiles offer opportunity for forming pattern through organization of different colors and glazes.

Laying tiles from light to dark, or intermixing cool and warm tones, creates visual rhythm. In his bathroom, Kaffe covered countertops and vanities with multicolored tiles, creating interesting plays of light and dark, bright and dull. He enhanced visual interest by varying the sizes of the tiles from one surface to another.

Opposite: Antique hand-beaded bags, one of Kaffe's favorite collectibles, beautifully complement the palette of blues and greens on a tiled surface.

Left and Below: Two sizes of tile in the bathroom provide double the impact. The lively rhythm created by placing tiles according to color is an ancient approach to pattern.

Cool Surfacing with Tile

How to place layer upon layer of pattern, color, and material within a single space without creating chaos? Kaffe's secret lies in careful, discreet integration of contrasting decorative elements into a unified whole. Each material, in some subtle way, relates to another in the space. Even a wall treatment as seemingly minor as a mosaic backsplash border in the kitchen was thoughtfully conceived. The watery blues, pale jade greens, and creamy white tiles echo the colors in the room's wallpaper—another Kaffe creation. And, the mosaic ties into collectibles on display in the room, especially Kaffe's favorite—blue and white English and Chinese pottery. One of the beauties in being something of a Renaissance artist like Kaffe is being able to inter-relate themes between various design mediums. Kaffe's kitchen wallpaper design featuring blue-and-white china relates to his mosaic tiles and, at an even more basic level, to the collectibles that inspired it.

Right: A ceramic tile backsplash topped with a small-tile mosaic border lends unity to the assortment of blue-and-white pottery pieces in the kitchen.

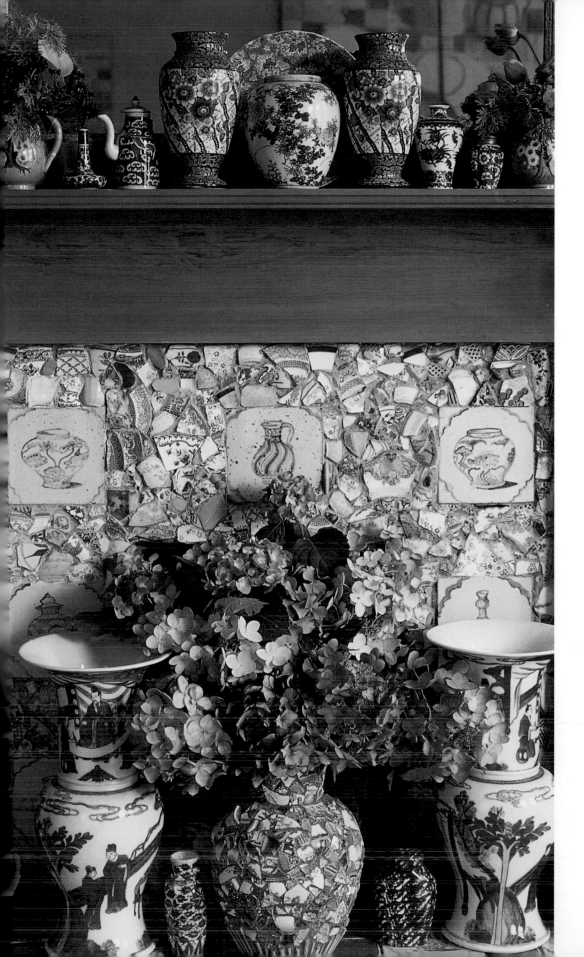

"You could call my style
'thoughtful kitsch' or
'embarrassment of riches'
or 'the more the merrier.'"

Even negative space is an invitation to
decorate to an eye as insightful as Kaffe's.
Using broken bits and pieces of pottery
he had gathered during strolls through
Hampstead Heath, he replaced the gaping
hole of his living room fireplace with a
mosaic fire screen. To add order to the
mishmash of pieces, Kaffe inset ceramic
tiles he painted with pottery motifs in
blue and white. The tiles provide a visual
connection to the blue-and-white vases,
urns, and other ceramics displayed on the
mantel shelf.

*Left: Handpainted tiles on the fire
screen repeat the forms of pottery
displayed on the hearth and mantel.
Kaffe gave an ordinary vase a facelift
with a hand-applied mosaic
treatment, then centered it on the
hearth to lend continuity to the tile-
and-mosaic fire screen just behind it.*

41

Making the Most of Mosaic

Some rooms lend themselves to the cool hand of tiles better than others. In the bathroom, tiles are especially welcome for their rugged durability and tolerance of water. But in Kaffe's bathroom, an ordinary application is out of the question. His bath, dressed top to bottom in white-and-cream mosaic tiles, gains extraordinary handcrafted style with little oddities such as tiny mirrors and teapot lids. Kaffe not only designed the mosaic himself, but he applied it as well, covering all four walls and the ceiling. Even when working with a monochromatic (single color) palette, Kaffe ensures depth by varying the shades and tones of his chosen color (in this case, neutral white-cream).

Opposite, Above, and Left: An Old World—even Moorish— ambience is formed in the bath by covering all surfaces in mosaics using irregularly shaped cream and white china shards. Kaffe included a special backsplash border behind the sink as part of the mosaic, and framed a mirror using darker-hued bits of tile.

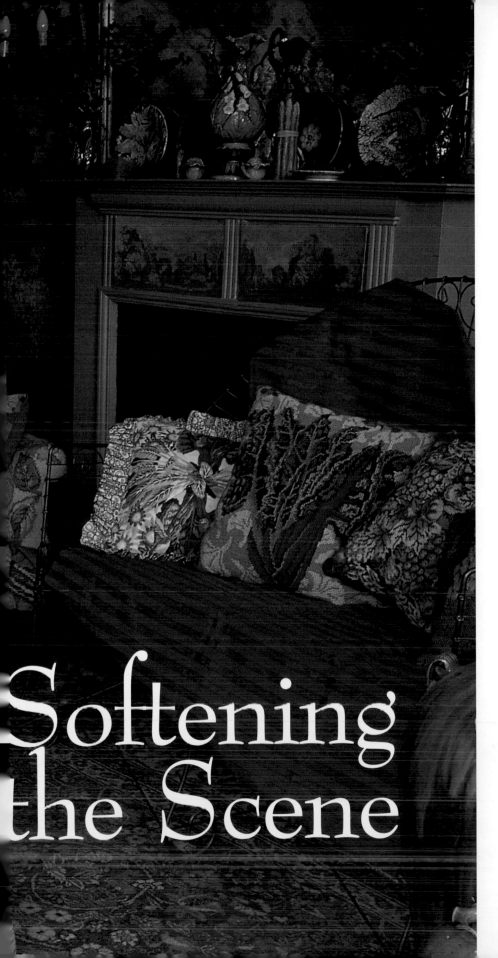

Softening
the Scene

How to get away with so many pattern combinations, so much color intensity, such a labyrinth of visual intrigue? One way is by softening the setting. And Kaffe is expert at it. He masterfully fills his rooms with sink-down upholstered furnishings and stacks of cushy pillows. Hard surfaces such as tabletops are softened with thick, quilted comfort. Hard walls are softened with fabric coverings and more—fabric- and paper-covered screens are positioned just so, transforming the walls into softer, three-dimensional surfaces.

Pattern and Color

Dining at Kaffe's place takes a natural course, with organic-motif fabrics featured center stage. Kaffe's popular chard design appears as the main fabric on the quilt covering the dining table. Then, it reappears on ruffled and needlepointed decorative pillows.

This use of the chard fabric in more than one way, and on more than one furnishing, helps to unify the multi-patterned room. Plus, what could be a more appropriate theme for a space intended to whet the appetite?

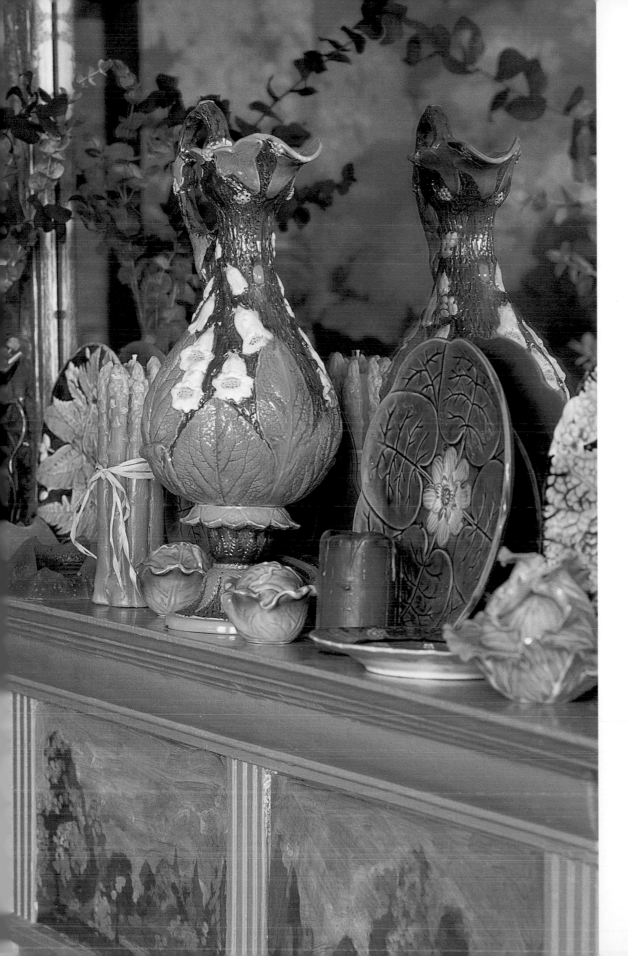

Left: An abundant harvest of fruit, vegetable, and flower motifs decorate Kaffe's dining room. Their patterns bind them together into an organic mix of fabric, needlepoint, majolica, and painted panels.

Opposite and Below: A chard motif unifies the dining room. The coordinating fabrics are part of Kaffe's popular patchwork-fabric range.

Pattern and Color

Kaffe doesn't ignore hard surfaces such as
ceramic collectibles, wood cabinets, or plaster
walls as areas for introducing color and pattern,
but it's the soft furnishings that make all his
efforts at color and pattern approachable.
A large pink rose motif splashed across a vivid
crimson background might intimidate with its
strong color and design—but not as a
needlepointed upholstery fabric for a chair.
Instead, what could be intimidating becomes
inviting. The needlepoint's pink roses are a
transitional thread connecting a mix of
patterns—from the pastel roses on the walls and
sofa to the exuberant floral pattern underfoot
on the rug.

"I do love to mix different

textiles, scales, and mediums if

the color and patterns relate.

I am always looking for

harmony in imperfect

juxtapositions. Mixtures bring

life to the color schemes."

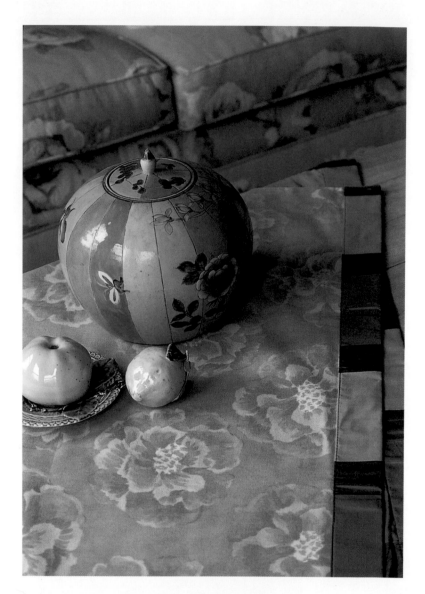

Above: *Fabric-on-fabric makes a soft bed for colorful ceramics,
while also providing transition between them and the floral fabric
on the living room sofa.*

Opposite: *The textural appeal of the flamboyant rag rug Kaffe
hooked softens the boldness of its design.*

Pattern and Color

Brightly colored flowers are a recurring theme Kaffe calls on throughout his home. Part of Kaffe's success in personalizing spaces lies in his unusual presentations. To introduce color and pattern, he groups flower-motif beaded bags in a big bowl. (Because of their exquisite hand-craftsmanship, as well as their looks, beaded bags form one of Kaffe's premier and prized collections.)

Another display unlike any other is Kaffe's still-life assortment of rose-themed fabrics, wrapping papers, tinware, porcelains, woven bags, books, and cards. Laid out with the front panels of a vest-in-the-making, the odds-and-ends pieces form a visually cohesive and pleasing arrangement.

Not one to be satisfied with a gorgeous but temporary arrangement, Kaffe continuously puts color pencils to paper to sketch a display that will last forever.

"I just love

overblown roses."

Opposite: *Beaded bags feature the same deep shadowing on flowers that Kaffe creates on his needlepoint designs.*

Left: *Two of the rose fragments in this pretty vignette are the front parts of a petit-point waistcoat Kaffe designed for his 1999 flower-theme show in New York City.*

51

Pattern and Color

Inspirations from nature as hard and solid as stone go soft around the edges with Kaffe's artistry, in the form of needlepoint pillows. He displays the inspiration and the art together, intensifying the character of each through contrast. Colors in the pillow's yarn palette are eminently stonelike—muted, the color of rain, yet subtly varied for a range of shades and tones within a monochromatic palette. Even here, where the look goes quiet and gray, nothing is quite as simple as it appears—nuances of color imbue depth and richness.

Right: The hard geometry of a living room corner is softened by a tabletop display including two needlepoint pillows of Kaffe's design. The painting just behind the table also is by Kaffe. This vignette illustrates Kaffe's adeptness at working within a monochromatic (single color), neutral palette.

Below: Kaffe's quilt and mosaic both have the muted coloration of age. He says: "I just put stuff together 'till they sing—if not, I try some other combination."

Taking inspiration from a Dutch
painting featured in Kaffe's book,
Glorious Inspirations, Kaffe's studio
workers hand-needlepointed both a
chair and stool in a strikingly beautiful
seashell motif. Shown in front of a
Kaffe painting that also features a
natural colorway with hints of yellow
and lavender, the needlepoint pattern
mixes seamlessly. Yet another textile—a
quilt mounted over the wall—brings a
smaller-scale geometric print to the
mix. Tiles on a tabletop echo that
geometry, and also the faded browns
and blues.

"I do love to mix different textiles,
scales, and mediums if the color and
patterns relate," says Kaffe. "I am always
looking for harmony in imperfect
juxtapositions. Mixtures bring life to
the color schemes."

*Left: A rusty-red background
on the antique area rug
accentuates the reddish hints
found in the painting and on
the chair fabric.*

53

Quilts, Pillows, and Rugs

In his bedroom, Kaffe leaves behind the glittering jewel tones and diverse pattern mixes for a soothing sensibility. Earthy colors—browns and rusts that look like they've faded over time or been sifted with a dusting of flour—decorate the space. And especially in this private cocoon, the softening touch of textiles is everywhere—from the schoolhouse quilt on the wall to the layered bed linens; from the decorative pillows to the well-worn geometry of the rug on the floor.

"Mixtures bring life

to color schemes."

Left: Piles of pillows soften the decor.
Opposite: The schoolhouse wall quilt features
Kaffe's fabrics. Kaffe hand-knitted the Tumbling
Blocks bed cover. The rag rug "Mischievous" is
by Brandon Mably.

Quilts, Pillows, and Rugs

A quick and easy way to soften spaces is with decorative throw pillows. Given Kaffe's fondness for changing the look of his rooms, the portability of pillows becomes especially attractive. Pillows can be tossed upon a chair to add instant color and pattern. But when that look bores, they can be tossed elsewhere (even in the closet) and replaced with others that strike an entirely different note. Because of their relatively small size, pillows also are ideal canvasses for displaying hand-craftsmanship. Kaffe's needlepoint patterns are particularly popular—in his own home, as well as among the public.

Above: Pillows in a stack—storage on a chair. A tower of pillows makes a fun fashion statement when the fabrics are as attractive as these—Kaffe's designs for Designers Guild.

Left: Richard Womersley, Kaffe's business partner, wove the throw that's covering the chair, providing a perfect perch for Kaffe's needlepoint Rooster pillow.

Opposite: One of Kaffe's favorite flowers, the gazania, decorates his fabric design, which covers pillows and is repeated in the quilt.

Softening the Scene Quilts, Pillows, and Rugs

Like the Jericho walls of the song, those in
Kaffe's home tumble down when covered
with Kaffe's Tumbling Blocks quilt. The
pattern cascades down the wall with intense
energy—energy heightened by a palette Kaffe
calls "full blooded." Rich and warm, it extends
to every other element within the quilt's
proximity: the chair, pillow, rag rug,
even the pot of flowers, seem to
radiate heat. By keeping all the
furnishings' fabrics the same
intensity, the vibrant mix succeeds.

"I just put stuff together 'till

they sing—if not, I try some

other combination."

*Right: The antique chair gets a new covering in
one of Kaffe's needlepoint patterns.*
*Opposite: This still life consists entirely of designs
by Kaffe, even including the rag rug. The Tumbling
Blocks Quilt is bordered in Kaffe's Indian Stripe
fabric. The pillow features a needlepoint center and a
crazy patchwork border.*

Creating the Mood

Any room can feature this wall color and that furniture fabric; this style of window treatment and that kind of sofa. So what's to distinguish one room from another—or, more to the point, someone's room from anyone else's? The answer lies in the personal details: a home needs to reflect the interests of its occupants. Professional interior designers know this well and take time to learn their client's preferences on the smallest level, for it's the only thing that saves even the best designs from looking canned. In Kaffe's home, one-of-a-kind personal details that attest to his passions abound—memorabilia from favorite places, collections reflecting his love for various forms or patterns. Every square inch within every room reveals some facet of Kaffe's taste, character, and talents, to make his living spaces sing.

Inspiring Collections

If collections are one of design's most important aspects, it's essential to know how to create them. Not all vases grouped en masse create a collection. Kaffe's definition of a collection, despite its apparent looseness, hinges on some concrete criteria. First, objects must relate in type—paintings displayed with paintings, china with china. But that's not all. His grouping must relate thematically—these are paintings of china, or of stones, for example. And to qualify as a collection of paintings

in one of Kaffe's rooms, the group also must relate in color—the palette of each painting must be compatible with those of the others.

But compatibility isn't entirely the answer: In terms of shape, variety is the better option. His canvases are a mixed bag of scale and shape, allowing the eye to dance around and better appreciate all the pieces within the grouping because of their diversity, not despite it.

Left: Here, Kaffe has hung a collection of paintings in, of all places, his textiles studio, because the room is long and therefore has more vista. Says Kaffe, "I can see at a glance how a show is shaping up, as I work on my textile projects."

Opposite: Kaffe's painting of a majolica still life, shown in the background, inspired this grouping of teapots and facilitiates the seamless transition from the wall to the objects on the table.

Teapots, as with his other collections, are acquired intuitively, not according to any prescribed plan. "Some find me as gifts, others I collect instinctively," he explains. Arranged together in layers, tiered by size, the teapots make teatime a conversation item, any time of day.

Inspiring Collections

Many of the collections giving unique character to
Kaffe's rooms have the Orient as either their origin or
their inspiration. This is mainly coincidental: it's not the
idea of the objects being oriental that counts with
Kaffe, as much as that they have an appealing design or
look. Blue and white colorations especially appeal to
him and they star in still lifes throughout his house.
Kaffe doesn't limit himself to two-tone ceramics,
though, as displayed in the rounded forms of smiling
Buddhas, with the Zen men issuing joy from a living
room window.

*Above: Most of Kaffe's smiling
Buddhas are more than 100 years old.*
*Left: Unity in color but diversity in
shape—a combination of English
and oriental china makes a strong
graphic statement.*

Color is the foundation for many of Kaffe's groupings of artful accessories. Blue is a favorite foundation—yet, as seen from these two examples, it can present strikingly different results. Blues, appreciated as solids with no other colors competing, go rich and oceany on art-glass pottery. The clean shapes of these bottles and vases are shown to their best advantage against a blue mosaic wall and tabletop

An entirely different mood is achieved by another grouping of blues that has a big temple jar as its focal point. The temple jar connects the disparate items in the group—a painting by Kaffe, as well as two temple jar needlepoint cushions and a swatch of temple-jar decorator fabric. "I know if I can paint something, I can justify the expense of buying it," says Kaffe. "This temple jar has figured in many tapestries, paintings, and fabric designs."

Left: The pattern on a blue temple jar is a favorite inspiration for many of Kaffe's designs.
Below: Echoes of the 1940s and 1950s can be seen in this blue themed vase collection.

Inspiring Collections

Adjusting a room's purpose presents no problem for Kaffe. What was once a bedroom now serves as his art studio. At certain times of day the light is perfect for carrying out painterly interpetations of one of his many collections, be it a selection of teapots, or a study in a pastel grouping of vases, bowls, and books.

It's interesting to note that at times a collection may inspire a painting, yet occasionally it's a painting that inspires another collection. Kaffe's vast store of vases, pots, and teapots allows him to mix and match to his heart's content in infinite combinations based on shape, color, or purpose.

Left: A small grouping of jars, vases, and books stars on a painting in progress. Their soft pastel colors proved to be the reason for their selection from the loaded cabinet.

"I know if I can paint
something, I can justify
the expense of buying it."

Left: A cabinet full of
decorative pots reflects
Kaffe's fondness for certain
shapes and patterns. Variety
in size, shape, and type
results in maximum visual
interest. The pots rest in full
view in Kaffe's painting
studio, waiting to star on his
canvasses. He uses them over
and over in his still lifes.

Accents and Accessories
Accents

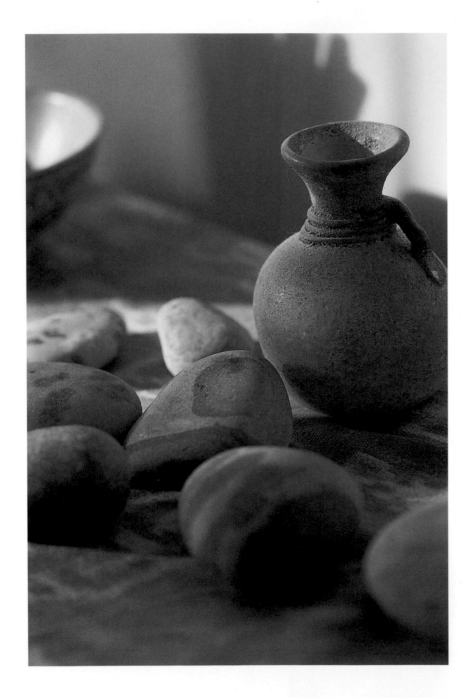

Even stones—or especially stones—are signature design pieces to Kaffe's discerning eye. And therefore they merit a place in his home as prized collectibles every bit as legitimate as any others. The subtle nuances of pattern and color in objects from nature render them as decorative as the more brightly colored and boldly patterned florals Kaffe designed as needlepoint patterns. The effect is the same: the stones bring individuality to their area of display; the needlepointed florals make each chair they cover a stand-out. What's more, the differences between the two types of objects only increase the home's vitality, pleasing the eye with a range of textures, palettes, and patterns.

Left: Murky mauves and grays on river stones appeal to Kaffe's appreciation for variegated color.

Above and Right: Faux-Roccoco chairs from a London flea market receive one-of-a-kind attention from Kaffe. Each is painted a different color and covered in a different (but related) needlepoint design. Kaffe's designs were stitched by David Forest.

Accents and Accessories

One of the most telling testaments to a person's taste isn't the decorative objects they put on obvious display, but the utilitarian items such as their everyday dinnerware. Even here, Kaffe holds true to form, revealing himself as an inveterate mixer with little regard for anything matched. "We have some sets of china in the house," he confesses, "but I do love a motley collection of compatible plates." And coffee mugs. And bowls. And saucers. And teapots. And so on. Instead of hiding the hodgepodge behind closed doors, Kaffe seizes the opportunity to decorate his kitchen. Everyday wares are stored on open shelving, becoming collections in their own right.

In addition to introducing inimitable character through major focal points, Kaffe zooms in on the details, too. No corner of anything—be it wall, mantel, or tabletop—is too small to serve as an opportunity to project personality. An example of decorating down to the details is a collection of inlaid-wood and flower-theme boxes at one corner of a table—pure Kaffe.

Opposite: Kaffe designed this deliberately mismatched set of dinnerware with well-known English potter Rupert Spira. The seashell oilcloth is also Kaffe's design.

Below: Kaffe's collection of boxes includes tin, marquetry, and Chinese parchment.

"Being a poor artist when I arrived in London, I bought cheap, broken, and damaged but very pretty, objects and placed them all together in pleasing arrangements—making still lifes actually."

Accents and Accessories

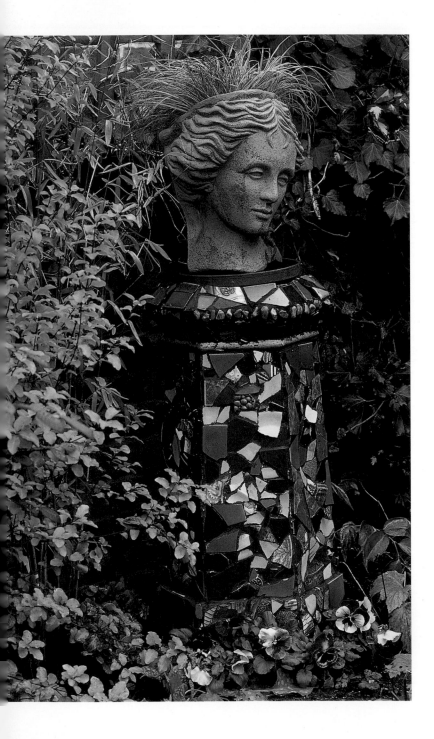

Not one to leave things halfway done, Kaffe tackles his small garden with as much gusto and ferver as he does his home. His chosen artform for this area, mosaic, allows him to create the patchwork-like look he enjoys working in the most. The inventive pieces stand up to the damp English climate and provide a splash of color during dreary days.

Large film cannister lids, a square of plywood, and a sewer pipe all have one thing in common—they're excellent surfaces for mosaic work.

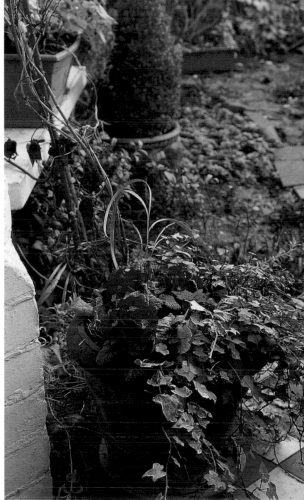

Opposite: A clay sewer pipe and the lid of a large film cannister provide exciting shapes for Kaffe's foray into mosaics.

Left: Leaning up against a tree, purple and yellow pansies artfully fill a plain wooden board. A sealer ensures protection against dampness.

Above: Tile walks, mosaic pots, and lots of flowers provide Kaffe with a restful outdoor area.

73

This museum retrospective of Kaffe's work looks familiar for good reason—many of the textile arts and accessories featured are plucked straight from his home.

Worldwide Influences

In 1988, the Victoria and Albert Museum in London hosted a retrospective exhibition of Kaffe's work, making him the first living textile artist to have a one-man show there. Since then, the show has traveled to Finland, Holland, Norway, Denmark, Sweden, Australia, and Canada. Finally, in 1998, it made its way to the USA. The images shown in this chapter are from the Minneapolis Institute of Fine Art, which presented the show in great detail. The layers of pattern and texture against the coral red background, below, reflect Kaffe's fascination with oriental richness. Opposite, needlepoint flowers and bold knits mix seamlessly with the museum's Chinese chair.

Life Imitates Art or Art Imitates Life?

In this case, the dividing line is blurred. The vignettes on these pages capture the essence of the exhibition, which is all about integrating Kaffe's textiles into realistic home settings. Much of the show's charm lies in the approachable, as opposed to museum-like, atmosphere of the capsuled displays. At the center of the exhibition is a true-to-life rendering of Kaffe's at-home London studio, complete with artful inspirations tacked to a pinboard (top right, below, and below right). Kaffe's fruit and vegetable needlepoint pillows snuggle up warmly on the museum's antique European sofa (opposite).

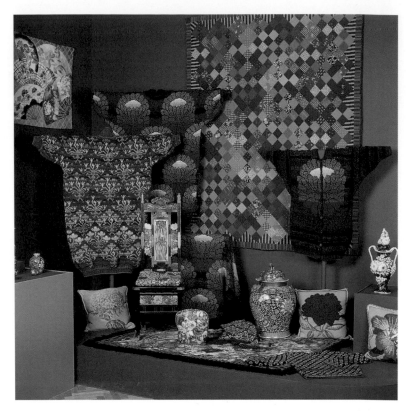

Geometric Harmony

Simple, yes, but there's nothing plain about these geometrically intriguing pieces. The designs are bold, with richly resonant color and crisp pattern repeats. The museum's displays follow that cue, with each textile sample stretched, folded, or mounted to accentuate its linear definition. Be it patchwork, knitting, or needlepoint, Kaffe's fondness for geometric structure is clearly evident.

The tweedy palette of the vignette shown opposite reflects Kaffe's response to the gray light of England. The sampler blanket contains some of his first attempts at taking the yarns and "playing with color!"

A Striking Blend
of Old and New

The museum staff's insight into Kaffe's work shows in every way. They custom-painted backgrounds for the various vignettes in eighteen different compatible colors (almost like home) and pulled just the right antique decorative pieces from the museum's archives to complement Kaffe's work. After all, so much of what Kaffe does is directly inspired by the history of decorative arts.

   The tropical flower needlepoint, above, blends beautifully with the Museum's Japanese jar while a periwinkle blue background sets off the red and blue knits, opposite.

Projects
and Creativity

1 yellow
2 Dk law
3 Lavender
4 ochre
5 green
pale blue

red
gold Band
gold rays stripes

84

very deep browns
ivory + gold Brownwood.
yellow? Dark
Ochre

Bright Turq.
jade green spots into yellowish ochre
green with Turq. edges
Browny black base.

Interpretations of collections, images, and patterns all come together in Kaffe's inspirational sketch books. Using watercolors and brushes, felt-tip pens or color pencils, he fills page after page with trials of a certain motif or color scheme until it's just right. Only then does the pattern get translated into a needlepoint canvas, large mock-up for a patchwork or decorator fabric, or quilt or rag rug design. Many of the quilts, rag rugs, and pillows shown in the photographs are featured in this chapter for you to make and enjoy.

Tumbling Blocks Quilt

Materials

- 45-inch-wide 100% cotton fabrics:
  1 fat quarter each of 8 different
      stripe fabrics
  2 yards of solid deep pink fabric for the
      background triangles
  4 yards of solid magenta fabric for the
      border pieces and backing
  1½ yards of stripe fabric for the outer
      border and bias binding
- Batting at least 3 inches larger all around
      than the finished quilt top
- Cotton quilting thread
- Templates A, B, C, and D on pages
    118–119

Size of Quilt

The finished Tumbling Blocks Quilt measures 54½ x 74 inches. Quilting will reduce the final measurements.

Shapes

The patchwork blocks are made from a single diamond shape (template A). The patchwork background between the tumbling blocks is made from a small equilateral triangle (template B). The equilateral triangles for the top and border edges are made from a small equilateral triangle (template B) and a trapezoid shape (template C). The side edges are made with a large elongated triangle (template D) The actual-size templates are given on pages 118–119.

Cutting

Template A: Cut 291 from stripe fat quarters.
Template B: Cut 210 from solid deep pink fabric.
Template C: Cut 16 from solid magenta fabric.
Template D: Cut 14 from solid magenta fabric.
For the outer border strips, cut enough 2½-inch-wide strips across the width of the fabric to piece together two 2½ x 55-inch strips for the top and bottom borders, and two 2½ x 70-inch strips for the side borders.
Cut a total of 8 yards of 3-inch-wide bias strips for the binding.

The classic tumbling blocks is a favorite pattern of Kaffe's and he uses it often in his knitting and quilting patterns. Quilters will enjoy the challenge of finding just the right fabrics needed to create the illusion of tumbling cubes.

Quilts and Instructions

Making the Blocks

Select three A diamonds from the variety you've cut. Arrange the three diamonds following the block assembly diagram, below.

Using the seam allowances marked on the templates, sew the left-hand diamond patches together, then stitch the right-hand diamond patch to the two joined patches using a set-in seam. Sew a B background triangle to the top and bottom of the cube (positioning the stripes at random).

Make a total of 97 diamond blocks.

Making the Top and Bottom Border Triangles

Referring to the border triangle diagram, below right, sew the remaining B triangles to the matching edges of the C trapezoids.

Sewing the Patches into Rows

Following the layout diagram, opposite, arrange the center of the quilt as follows: Select two tumbling blocks and arrange them in a diagonal row; sew together. Take four tumbling blocks and arrange them in the next diagonal row; sew together.

Continue in this manner, arranging and sewing subsequent diagonal rows of 6, 8, 10, 12, 13, 12, 10, 8, 6, 4, and 2 tumbling blocks until there are a total of 13 rows.

Referring to the layout diagram, sew a border triangle to the top of each of the first seven rows. Sew a border triangle to the bottom of the seventh row. Then sew the remaining bottom border triangles to the bottom of rows 8–13.

Referring to the layout diagram, sew a magenta D triangle to the bottom of each of the first six rows, skip the seventh row, then sew a triangle to the top of each of rows 8-13. Sew the two remaining D triangles to the two remaining border triangles for the top left and bottom right corners.

Assembling the Rows

Following the layout diagram, join the diagonal rows. Then join the top left and bottom right corners. Sew the long border strips to the side edges of the pieced panel; trim the ends even with the edges of the panel. Sew the shorter border strips to the top and bottom edges of the pieced panel; trim the ends.

Finishing the Quilt

Press the pieced quilt top. Layer the quilt top, batting, and backing, and baste the layers.

Quilt in the ditch in the border seams. Then stipple-quilt the background triangles.

Trim the quilt edges and attach the binding.

Block Assembly Diagram

Border Triangle Diagram

Tumbling Blocks Layout Diagram

Blue Star Quilt

Materials

- 45-inch-wide 100% cotton fabrics:
  1 fat quarter each of 11 different
    stripe fabrics
  1 yard of solid medium blue fabric for
    the background
  1 yard of red wide-stripe fabric for the
    bias binding
  1 yard of multicolored narrow-stripe
    fabric for the inner border
  1 yard of multicolored wide-stripe
    fabric for the outer border
  4½ yards of solid deep blue fabric for the
    background and backing
- Batting at least 3 inches larger all around
    than the finished quilt top
- Cotton quilting thread
- Templates E, F, and G on pages 120–121

Size of Quilt

The finished Blue Star Quilt measures 62 x 90 inches. Quilting will slightly reduce the final measurements.

Shapes

The patchwork blocks are made from a large diamond (template E). The background pieces between the stars are the same large diamonds (template E). The large pieces for the top and bottom edges are made from a house-shape piece (template G). The side edges are finished with a trapezoid shape (template F). The actual-size templates are given on pages 120–121.

Cutting

Template E: Cut 378 from the striped fat quarters, having the stripes run lengthwise with template.

Template E: Cut 82 from solid medium blue fabric and 83 from solid deep blue fabric.

Template F: Cut 20 from narrow-stripe fabric.

Template G: Cut 7 from narrow-stripe fabric.

Wow! What a fun way to play with striped fabrics! One of the "labor of love" quilts we sometimes hear about, this one's absolutely worth the effort. The graphic effect is dazzling, and the deep, gorgeous colors take on a starring role.

Quilts and Instructions

From the multicolored wide stripe fabric for the outer border strips, cut enough 2½-inch-wide strips across the width of the fabric to piece together two 2½ x 64-inch strips for the top and bottom edges, and two 2½ x 86-inch strips for the side edges.

From the red wide-stripe fabric, cut a total of 9 yards of 3-inch-wide bias strips for the binding.

Making the Stars

Select two groups of three same-fabric E diamonds from the variety you've cut. Referring to the star assembly diagram, below, arrange the six diamonds, alternating the fabrics.

Using the seam allowances marked on the templates, sew the top three diamond patches together, sew the bottom three diamond patches, then stitch the two sets together. Make a total of 63 stars.

Adding the Blue Background Diamonds

Sew a blue E diamond to the bottom of 56 of the stars. Sew two blue E diamonds to each side of 24 of the 56 stars. You will have seven plain stars remaining.

Sewing the Stars into Rows

Following the layout diagram, opposite, and referring to the color photograph on page 91, arrange the stars in seven vertical rows of nine stars each, until you have a pleasing composition, making sure the last star in each row is a plain star. Arrange the rows so they're off-set and fit into each other nicely.

Referring to the layout diagram, sew a blue E diamond to the top of rows 1, 3, 5, and 7, and to the bottom of rows 2, 4, and 6. Also sew a blue E diamond to each side of the bottom stars of rows 2, 4, and 6. When you're completely satisfied with the arrangement, sew the stars together into seven vertical rows.

Assembling the Rows

Following the layout diagram, join the vertical rows.

Adding Inner Border Pieces

Following the layout diagram, sew the narrow-stripe G pieces between the stars at the top and bottom edges of the quilt top. Sew the narrow-stripe F pieces between the stars at the side edges. Trim the excess fabric from the corner pieces.

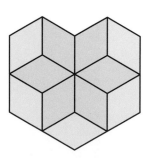

Star Assembly Diagram

Adding the Outer Border Strips

Sew the long border strips to the side edges of the pieced panel, trim the ends even with the edges of the panel. Sew the shorter border strips to the top and bottom edges of the pieced panel; trim the ends.

Finishing the Quilt

Press the pieced quilt top. Layer the quilt top, batting, and backing, and baste the layers.

Meander-quilt the narrow-stripe inner border pieces. Stipple-quilt the blue background diamonds.

Trim the quilt edges and attach the binding.

Star Layout Diagram

Quilts and Instructions
Quilts

Kaffe's Garden Quilt

Materials

- 45-inch-wide 100% cotton fabrics:
  10 yards of directional print★
  4 yards of floral print
  4 yards of green print
  2 yards of gray print
  1 yard of brown print
  12 yards of stripe fabric for triangles, bias
      binding, and backing
- Batting at least 3 inches larger all around
      than the finished quilt top
- Cotton quilting thread
- Templates H and I on pages 122–123

★ The placement of the directional print is
critical to the look of the quilt. While this
takes more fabric than usual, it gives the
quilt its exciting movement.

Size of Quilt
The finished Kaffe's Garden Quilt measures 93 x 115
inches. Quilting will reduce the final measurements.

Shapes
Block 1 is made from a 5-inch square shape and a house
shape (template I).

Block 2 is made from a 5-inch square shape, a 7-inch
square shape, and a 5 x 7-inch rectangle shape.

Block 3 and Triangle 4 are made from a triangle shape
(template H).

The actual-size templates H and I are given on pages
122–123.

Cutting
Note: When cutting the fabrics, pay very close attention
to the color photograph, opposite. The placement of the
directional print is critical.

For the inner border strips, cut enough 5-inch-wide
    strips across the width of the fabric to piece together
    two 5 x 95-inch strips of floral print fabric for the top
    and bottom edges, and two 5 x 117-inch strips of flo-
    ral print fabric for the side edges.

A perfect creation for
Kaffe's leafy dining
room, this large quilt
sports fabrics in garden
colors and motifs.
The fabrics are cut in
such a way as to utilize
the patterns to their
greatest advantage.

Quilts and Instructions

For the outer border strips, cut enough 7½-inch-wide strips across the width of the fabric to piece together two 7½ x 95-inch strips of directional print fabric for the top and bottom edges, and two 7½ x 117-inch strips of directional print fabric for the side edges.

Cut forty-eight 5-inch squares from floral-print fabric.

Cut sixteen 5 x 7-inch rectangles from directional print fabric.

Template H: Cut 24 from green print fabric, ten from gray print fabric, and 14 from stripe fabric.

Template I: Cut 32 from directional print fabric.

Cut four 7-inch squares from brown print fabric.

From the stripe fabric, cut a total of 12 yards of 3-inch-wide bias strips for the binding.

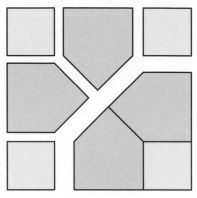

Block 1 Diagram

Making the Blocks and Triangles

Referring to the diagrams, right and opposite, construct eight of Block 1, four of Block 2, five of Block 3, and 14 of Triangle 4. Each block should measure 15½ inches square, not including seam allowances.

Sewing the Blocks and Triangles into Rows

Before sewing the Blocks and Triangles together, they need to be placed in proper position. It's best to do this on a clean floor in an area that doesn't see much, or any, traffic because you may have to leave the pieces on the floor for a few days. It is important to lay out all the blocks and triangles on the floor first, before doing any sewing—the success of the quilt hinges on the precise placement of the parts.

Following the layout diagram, opposite, arrange the quilt in diagonal rows as follows: For Row 1, select two Triangle 4 units and place together. For Row 2, select a Block 2 and a Block 3 and place together. Place a Triangle 4 at each end.

Block 2 Diagram

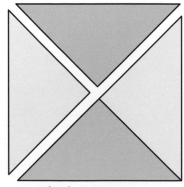

Block 3 Diagram

Continue to add diagonal rows, referring to the layout diagram for placement. If at all possible, take a picture of your composition and compare it to the photograph on page 95.

When you are completely satisfied, sew the parts together one row at a time, picking up only the blocks and/or triangles you are sewing together, and not all the blocks/triangles for an entire row.

Assembling the Rows

Following the layout diagram, join the diagonal rows.

Adding the Borders

Referring to the photograph on page 95, sew the floral print and directional print border strips together in matching pairs, sewing along one long edge and making sure the directional print fabric is facing the same way in each pair. Sew the short pairs to the top and bottom edges of the quilt top and the long pairs to the side edges. Miter the corners.

Finishing the Quilt

Press the pieced quilt top. Layer the quilt top, batting, and backing, and baste the layers.

Quilt in the ditch in all the main block and triangle seams.

Trim the quilt edges and attach the binding.

Kaffe's Garden Layout Diagram

Triangle 4 Diagram

Quilts and Instructions
Quilts

Schoolhouse Quilt

Size of Quilt

The finished Schoolhouse Quilt measures 63 x 89 inches. Quilting will slightly reduce the final measurements.

Note

To make the front of each house stand out, Kaffe turned the fabrics over and used the backside, except the stripe fabric, which he turned from vertical to horizontal.

Shapes

The Schoolhouse blocks all use the same shapes. The actual-size templates J, K, and L are on pages 124–125.

Cutting

Note: The Schoolhouse blocks at first glance look to be good candidates for strip piecing; however, because of the variety in color it's easier to use the templates and cut all pieces individually. There are 24 blocks: Six of multicolored large print, six of stripe, six of floral print, and six of multicolored small print A fabric.

From each of the four block fabrics, cut six pieces K, six pieces L, and nine 2-inch-wide strips across the width of the fabric; from these strips, cut thirty 7½-inch lengths M and forty-two 2½-inch lengths N.

Kaffe has managed to rework an old (and sometimes tired) pattern into a breath of fresh air.

By using the right side as well as the wrong side of his fabrics, he's lent a dimensionality to the houses, giving the pattern a whole new twist.

Quilts and Instructions

From solid tan fabric, cut eight 2-inch-wide strips across the width of the fabric; from these strips, cut forty-eight 3½-inch lengths O and twenty-four 5½-inch lengths P. Cut seven 2½-inch-wide strips across the width of the fabric; from these strips, cut twenty-four 4¼-inch lengths Q, twenty-four 3½-inch lengths R, and twenty-four 2¾-inch lengths S. Cut two 3½-inch-wide strips across the width of the fabric; from these strips, cut 24 pieces J and 24 pieces Jr.

From multicolored small print B fabric, cut ten 2-inch-wide strips across the width of the fabric; from these strips cut twenty-eight 12½-inch lengths for the horizontal lattice. Cut two 12½-inch-wide strips across the width of the fabric; from these strips cut thirty 2-inch lengths for the vertical lattice.

From the floral print fabric, cut thirty-five 2-inch squares for the lattice corner blocks, trying to place a flower motif in the center of each square.

For the border strips, cut enough 4½-inch-wide strips across the width of the fabric to piece together two 4½ x 60-inch strips of brown print fabric for the top and bottom edges and two 4½ x 86-inch strips of brown print fabric for the side edges. Cut four 4½-inch squares for the border corner blocks.

From the multicolored small print B fabric, cut a total of 9 yards of 3-inch-wide bias strips for the binding.

Making the Blocks

The Schoolhouse blocks are all made in the same manner but in four different colorways.

Referring to the Schoolhouse block diagram, sew the N pieces to each end of the O pieces. Sew the resulting strips to three M strips, alternating the strips. For the front of the house, sew an N piece to one end of a P piece, making sure the N piece will face wrong side up in the pieced strip. Sew the resulting strip between two M strips, making sure the M strips will face wrong sides up.

Sew the front of the roof K piece to the side roof L

piece, making sure the K piece will face wrong side up. Sew a J and Jr piece to each end of the roof. Sew this unit to the side and front wall unit, carefully matching the seams.

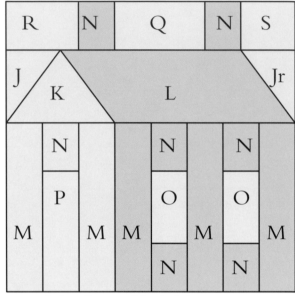

Schoolhouse Block Diagram

Sew the chimney N pieces to each end of the Q piece; sew the R piece to the left end and the S piece to the right end of the chimney unit.

Make a total of 24 Schoolhouse blocks.

Adding the Lattice Strips

Following the layout diagram, opposite, sew a vertical lattice strip to the left side of each block. Take five corner pieces and four horizontal lattice pieces and sew together into a strip. Make a total of seven such strips.

Sewing the Blocks into Rows

Following the layout diagram, opposite, arrange the center portion of the quilt, making sure the blocks are placed in the correct sequence and placing the lattice strips between the rows.

When you've checked and double-checked the correct placement, pick up the first two neigboring blocks of each horizontal row, and sew together. Pick up the next block and sew to the unit. Repeat across, then sew a vertical lattice strip to the end of the row. Repeat for the remaining rows.

Sew the block rows and the lattice rows together, carefully matching the seams.

Assembling the Rows

Following the layout diagram, sew the block rows and the lattice rows together, carefully matching the seams.

Adding the Borders

Sew the long border strips to the side edges of the quilt top. Sew the border corner blocks to the ends of the short border strips, turning the squares so the print runs in a different direction from the strips. Sew the strips to the top and bottom edges of the quilt top.

Finishing the Quilt

Press the pieced quilt top. Layer the quilt top, batting, and backing; baste the layers.

Quilt in the ditch in all the seams. Then meander quilt the lattice strips.

Trim the quilt edges and attach the binding.

Schoolhouse Layout Diagram

Toile Baby Quilt

Materials

- 45-inch-wide 100% cotton fabrics:
  ½ yard each of five different color toiles: teal, burgundy, rust, light green, and navy
  1¼ yards of solid beige fabric
  3 yards of stripe fabric for the bias binding and backing fabric
- Batting at least 3 inches larger all around than the finished quilt top
- Cotton quilting thread

Size of Quilt

The finished Toile Baby Quilt measures 63 x 89 inches. Quilting will slightly reduce the final measurements.

Shapes

The center of the quilt is made up of six 9-inch blocks surrounded by 2¼-inch blocks (finished sizes). The center has a border made with 4½-inch strips. A 2¼-inch block border surrounds the entire quilt.

Cutting

From green and burgundy toile fabrics, cut one 9½-inch strip and one 2¼-inch strip each across the widths of the fabrics. Cut one 9½-inch square each from the wide strips, then cut three 2¼-inch-wide strips each across the 35-inch widths of the remaining fabrics.

From teal and rust toile fabrics, cut one 9½-inch strip and two 2¼-inch strips each across the widths of the fabrics. Cut two 9½-inch squares each from the wide strips, then cut three 2¼-inch-wide strips across the 35-inch widths of the remaining fabrics.

What can you do with one patterned fabric? A lot, if you're using five colorways of the same one-pattern fabric! No strip-piecing here, just good old-fashioned "placing the colors where they look good" kind of piecing. The result is well worth the time, and baby will have a future heirloom.

Quilts and Instructions

From navy toile fabric, cut three 2¾-inch strips across the width of the fabric.

From the stripe fabric, cut a total of 8½ yards of 2¾-inch-wide bias strips for the binding.

From solid beige fabric, cut fifteen 2¾-inch strips.

Making the Square and Rectangle Segments

Sew a beige strip to each toile strip. From the resulting strip units, cut thirty-one 2¾-inch-wide segments and seven 5-inch-wide segments of each color. You will have a total of thirty-five 5-inch-wide segments; thirty-four are needed for this project.

Making the Quilt Sections

Sew two 2¾-inch-wide segments together into a four-square block, alternating the beige squares. Make a total of 22 blocks. Set four blocks aside for the inner border corner blocks.

Sew the remaining 18 blocks together into nine strips of two blocks each. These are the vertical sashing strips.

Referring to the layout diagram, opposite, sew fourteen 2¾-inch segments into a strip, alternating the beige squares. Repeat three times, varying the placement of the toile colors. These are the horizontal sashing strips.

Referring to the layout diagram, sew ten 5-inch segments into a long strip; repeat. Sew seven 5-inch segments into a strip; repeat. These are the inner border strips.

Referring to the layout diagram, sew ten 2¾-inch-wide segments together the long way. Repeat. These are the top and bottom borders. Sew twelve 2¾-inch-wide segments together the long way. Repeat once. These are the side borders.

Sewing the Units into Rows

Following the layout diagram, opposite, arrange the center of the quilt as follows: Select two large blocks and three vertical sashing strips, and arrange them in a horizontal row; sew together. Repeat two more times.

Assembling the Rows

Following the layout diagram, place the horizontal sashing strips between the rows and at the top and bottom of the unit. Sew together.

Sew the long inner border strip to the side edges of the center unit.

Sew a four-block square to each end of each shorter inner border strip. Sew the strips to the top and bottom edges of the center unit.

Sew the long border strips to the side edges of the center unit; sew the shorter border strips to the top and bottom edges of the center unit.

Finishing the Quilt

Press the pieced quilt top. Layer the quilt top, batting, and backing, and baste the layers.

Quilt in the ditch in the border seams. Then stipple- or meander-quilt as desired.

Trim the quilt edges and attach the binding.

Toile Layout Diagram

Pillows
Pillows and Instructions

Great accessories are easy to come by—just make an extra block while you're making your quilt. From your fabric leftovers, cut circles for a yo-yo pillow, or strips for a bright border.

Materials

- Scraps of many different quilt fabrics
- ½ yard of fabric for the back
- Polyester pillow form
- Cotton quilting thread

Size of Pillow

The size of your pillow will depend on the size of the additional quilt block and any borders you may wish to add. Piping and ruffles add additional inches.

Fabrics and Color

The fabrics used for the pillow blocks are the same as you use for your quilt blocks. Choose a matching fabric for the backing. Leftover fabrics are great for covering piping cord, piecing a scrap border, or making yo-yos.

Shapes

The shape of the quilt blocks largely determines the shape of the pillow. Keep in mind that a purchased pillow or pillow form is easiest to work with—borders can be added until the right shape is achieved.

Cutting the Fabrics

Depending on the pillow you choose to make, either cut the pieces needed for one quilt block from the Garden Quilt or Schoolhouse Quilt, or cut forty-nine 5-inch circles from a variety of scraps. Keep some matching fabrics on hand for borders, piping, and/or ruffles.

Making the Pillow Top

Refer to the quilt instructions to make your pillow block. For yo-yos, turn under the hem of each fabric circle and sew a running stitch all around the outer edge. Making sure the right side of the fabric is the outside of the yo-yo, gently pull the thread, gathering the fabric until a small opening is left. Knot the thread. Working from the center out, attach the yo-yos to each other and onto a large square of fabric.

Finishing the Pillow

Add borders until the pillow top is the desired size. Cover piping cord with a strip of fabric or cut a ruffle twice the length of the circumference of the pillow. Sew the piping or ruffle around the right side of the pillow top.

For the pillow back, cut a piece of fabric in the same height but 5 inches wider than the widest part of the pillow. Cut the fabric in half and hem the cut edges with 1-inch hems. With right sides together and outer edges matching, sew the back pieces to the pillow top, overlapping the hemmed edges neatly in the center. Turn the pillow right side out and insert the pillow form.

Rag Rug Patterns and Instructions

Rag Rugs

Leaves Rug

Deep autumn-colored leaves form a
border around a bright blue pond
splashed with floating lily pads.

Rag Rugs

Because of the large individual loops and the simple
hooking action, rag rugs are very quick to work. Begin
with a simple one such as the Blocks rug, or dive into a
somewhat more challenging one. Any one you choose
will be a joy to work up due to the basic techniques
described below. Rug hooking couldn't be simpler!

The materials that go into a rag rug are a good selection of scrap fabrics for your rag strips and a large piece
of burlap for the rug foundation.

General Instructions

The instructions for each rug are identical, except for the measurements. Read through all instructions thoroughly before starting your rug.

Foundation Fabric

Burlap is the best foundation fabric for rag rugs. It provides a strong base and the threads are wide apart enough to accommodate the rug hook. Kaffe normally uses a heavy-weight, loose weave burlap with about 10 or 11 threads to the inch. When you purchase your burlap be sure to add 5-inch margins (10 inches total) to your width and length measurements.

Rug Hooks

The main tool you need for hooking a rag rug is a rug hook. Basically, there are two types of hooks—one with a latch and one without. Kaffe prefers working with the latch hook because it is easy to use. The latch is pushed upward when the hook is inserted down through the fabric and then pulled down as the hook is pulled up through the fabric, enclosing the rag strip. The opening and closing action of the latch prevents the hook from catching on the burlap.

Leaves Rug finished size: 27 x 45 inches

Rag Rug Patterns and Instructions

Roses Rug

A favorite design subject, the rose takes

center stage on this fun-to-make rug.

A scallop border contains the growth.

Rug Frames

Kaffe does not use a frame when hooking a rug. This makes the project portable and allows him to move around within the design, filling in various areas without having to reframe each time. He says: "My finished rugs may not be as absolutely rectangular as a rug worked in a frame, but this slight asymmetry is part of the charm of the hand-hooked rag rug."

If you prefer to use a frame, a large artist's stretcher frame will do the trick. Use thumb tacks to secure the section of burlap you are working on to the stretcher.

Choosing the Colors

Study the photograph of the rug to decide which colors to choose. You will need scrap fabrics in a wide variety of colors and in a range of tones. Look for scraps to match the photographed color scheme or match the colors to your home decor.

Picking the Fabrics

Most fabric scraps are suitable for rag rug strips. Rag rugs are great recycling projects. Save old clothes for a rug with built-in memories or pick up inexpensive garments at rummage sales and thrift shops.

Patterned fabrics are just as enjoyable to work with as plain, and they often produce a lovely mottled effect. Don't restrict your choice of fabric to a specific thick-ness or texture either. Varying textures and fabric weights adds interest to the allover design and keeps it from being too uniform. Kaffe tends to collect fabrics that go well with a specific color palette. But try to find a wide variety of colors in a range of dark, medium, and light tones. With a good selection on hand, you will be able to pick and choose suitable colors as your design progresses.

To make sure all your scrap fabrics are preshrunk before use, wash and dry them before cutting strips. If you have not been able to locate fabrics in some of the colors you need, you may want to dye some of the scraps beforehand.

Roses Rug finished size: 39 x 63 inches.
Instructions begin on page 108.

111

Rag Rug Patterns and Instructions

Blocks Rug

A study in color doesn't need to be

boring. Pull many fabrics that belong to

the same color family and have at it.

Preparing the Rag Strips

The width of the rag strip depends on the texture you want in your rug, the thickness of the scrap fabric, the size of your rug hook, and the weight of the burlap. The best thing to do is to cut a short strip of fabric and hook a few test loops. In general, Kaffe cuts his rag strips between ½ inch and 1 inch wide—the thicker the fabric the narrower the strip should be.

In general, cut the strips on the straight grain of the fabric, not on the bias; however, for a long continuous strip, start cutting along an outside edge and cut in a decreasing spiral toward the center of the fabric.

Transferring the Design

Trace or copy the rag rug diagram of your choice. Using a pencil and ruler, divide the traced diagram in half horizontally and vertically, making equal quarters. Divide each quarter into smaller quarters.

Using dressmaker's chalk or a large needle with a long length of yarn, mark off the design area on the burlap, drawing only the outer outline to ensure a margin of burlap around your design area. Then divide the burlap design area the same way you did the diagram.

There are three methods to get the design onto the burlap: You can freehand-draw the design onto the burlap; draw the enlarged design directly onto the burlap square by square; or draw the design onto tracing paper, then transfer it to the burlap by using a hot-iron transfer pencil.

To copy the diagram square by square, use a felt-tip marker to copy an enlarged version of the diagram's design lines onto the burlap, following the diagram. Complete all the lines in one section before moving on to the next. Do not worry about making mistakes or corrections—the lines will be covered by the dense loops.

If you choose to enlarge the design on tracing paper, use a pencil to draw the outline and grid. To transfer the design from the tracing paper, first turn the paper over and, with a transfer pencil, retrace the center outline of the rug and the design lines (not the grid). Place the tracing paper on the burlap with the transfer-pencil side down. Using a hot iron, press the design onto the burlap following the instructions that come with the transfer pencil.

Blocks Rug finished size: 27 x 45 inches.
Instructions begin on page 108.

Rag Rug Patterns and Instructions

Mischievous Rug

Brandon Mably, Kaffe's business manager,

is a designer in his own right, as attested

by Mischievous the striped cat.

Hooking the Rug

Learning to hook a rug will take no time at all, especially when you use a latch hook. If you have never made a rag rug before, practice hooking on a scrap piece of burlap to determine the best widths for your strips and to decide on the height of the loops. Don't worry about making mistakes—you can pull the loops out if you make a mistake. After a completed rug has been walked on, it will be much harder to pull the loops out because the flattening of the rug pushes the loops together.

Some rug hookers prefer to work the loops underneath the burlap and some prefer the loops on top. Kaffe prefers to hook his loops on the topside of the burlap so he can see the design and color scheme materialize as he works.

If you are right handed, hold the hook in your right hand above the burlap and hold the rag strip in your left hand under the burlap. Lefties must reverse this action. Push the hook straight down through the burlap, making sure the entire latch goes through the fabric as well. Catch the fabric strip with the hook, enclose it with the latch, and pull the end of the strip through the fabric. Then insert the hook one or two fabric threads away from where it was first inserted. Pull the strip through again, this time forming a ¼- to ⅜-inch loop on the right side of the burlap. Continue making loops in this way, placing the loops close together but not overly tight. Kaffe's rugs generally have about seven loops to 2 inches.

When you come to the end of a strip or when you want to change colors, merely pull the end up to the right side of the fabric. Start the next strip about two fabric threads away from where the last strip ended. Do not insert the hook through the same hole as a previous loop or strip end or you might pull out a loop by accident. Trim the ends of the strips so they're the same height as the loops.

Which direction to work in is a matter of choice. Kaffe usually follows the shape of the design. For instance, on the Blocks Rug the loops are worked in straight lines, but on the Rose Rug the curved shapes are filled in with loops at random or in curves that follow the design line.

Finishing the Rug

A special advantage of rag rug making is that very little finishing is required. After completing the hooking, simply turn under the unworked burlap margins and hem, mitering the corners in the process. If desired, you can bind the rug with wide twill binding: trim the unworked edges to 2 inches and sew the twill binding next to the loops. Turn the binding to the wrong side and handsew in place with strong thread.

Mischievous Rug finished size: 34 x 41 inches.
Instructions begin on page 108.

Mosaics and Instructions
Mosaics

Materials

- Mosaic base of your choice, such as a plain vase, terra-cotta pot, or piece of plywood
- A variety of ceramic tiles, glass tiles, plates, cups, etc. Damaged goods are easy to find.
- Tile nippers
- Hammer
- Quick-setting floor- and wall-tile adhesive and grout or a premixed adhesive/grout product
- Protective eye covering

Breaking the Pieces

Using nippers, cut pieces from china plates, cups, etc. With the nippers you can actually cut small motifs from the china that you can then form into a pattern. To break tile, place between two towels on a board; tap gently with hammer.

Adhering to Base

An easy method for creating mosaics is to use a premixed product that combines adhesive and grout. Use it to secure pieces to the base, and to fill gaps between pieces. For delicate work, secure the shards with adhesive first, allow to dry, then apply grout. For a richer look, color grout with ink before using. Work grout between the pieces with a palette knife, then apply more grout with a damp cloth, wiping over entire surface for a smooth look. After the grout has partially set, wipe off excess with a clean, damp cloth. When grout is dry, polish shards with a paper towel. Apply a sealer, if necessary, to protect project from dampness.

China shards and broken tiles are turned into colorful accent pieces under Kaffe's talented hands.

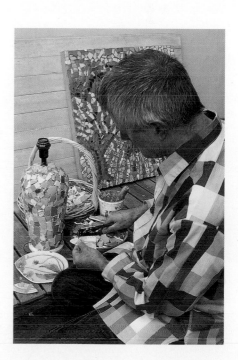

Quilt Patterns

Tumbling Blocks Quilt

A

B

C

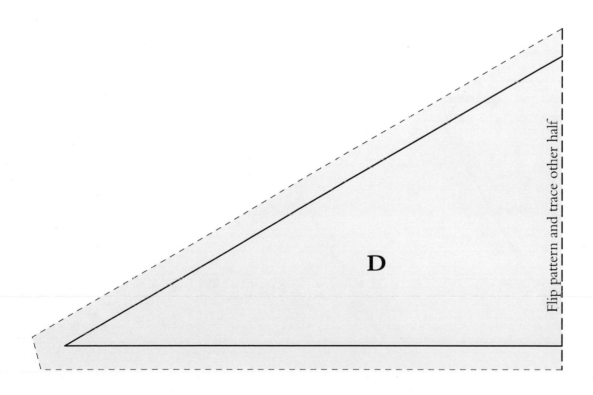

D

Flip pattern and trace other half

Quilt Patterns

Blue Star Quilt

E

F

Flip pattern and trace other half

Flip pattern and trace other half

G

Quilt Patterns

Kaffe's
Garden
Quilt

H

Flip pattern and trace other half

I

Quilt Patterns

Schoolhouse Quilt

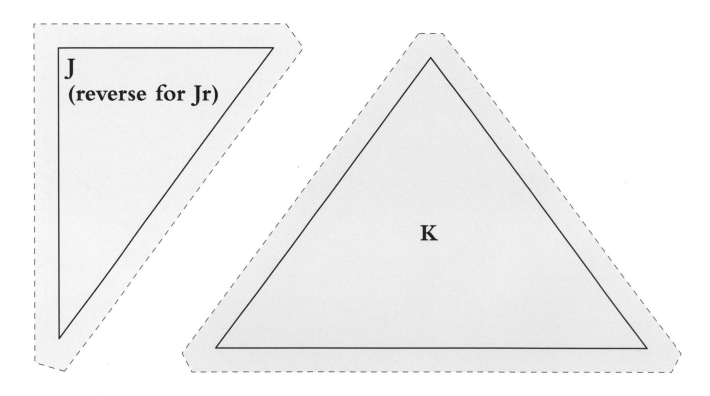

J
(reverse for Jr)

K

L

Acknowledgments

I would like to acknowledge with gratitude the people and organizations who helped me with my contribution to this book:

Lotus Stack, Liza Prior Lucy, Pauline Smith, Yvonne Edwards, Belinda Mably, Brandon Mably, Marlene Heuertz, Marjon Schaefer, Landauer Corporation, Margaret Sindelar, Barbara Dickerson, Roxanne LeMoine, Westminster Fibers, Ehrman, Rowan, and Designers Guild.

A special thank you to Debbie Patterson for her photography.

Kaffe Fassett

BOOKS BY KAFFE FASSETT:
Glorious Knits
Glorious Needlepoint
Family Album
Glorious Colour
Kaffe's Classics
Glorious Inspirations
Glorious Interiors
Glorious Patchwork
Mosaics

The fabrics used in the Tumbling Blocks and Blue Star quilts are Kaffe Fassett's Indian Stripe fabrics.

The fabrics used in the pillows and in the Schoolhouse and Kaffe's Garden quilts are Kaffe Fassett's Indian Stripe, Chard, Gazania, Roman Glass, Beads, and Pebbles fabrics.

Where to Buy

PATCHWORK FABRICS AND KITS:

WESTMINSTER FIBERS,
5 Northern Boulevard,
Amherst, NH 03031,
U.S.A.
Tel: (603) 886-5041,
Fax: (603) 886-1056.
ROWAN, Green Lane Mill,
Holmfirth, Huddersfield,
West Yorkshire HD7 1RW,
U.K.
Tel: (44) (1484) 681 881,
Fax: (44) (1484) 687 920.

NEEDLEPOINT KITS:

U.S.A.: *EHRMAN TAPESTRY,* 5300 Dorsey Hall Drive,
Suite 110, Ellicott City, MD 21042. Tel: toll-free order line
(888) 826-8600, customer service (410) 884-7944.
Fax: (410) 884-0598. E-mail: usehrman@mail.clark.net
U.K.: *EHRMAN (SHOP),* t14–16 Lancer Square, Kensington
Church Street, London W8 4EH, England.
Shop tel: (44) (171) 937 8123, Telephone ordering:
(44) (181) 573 4891, Fax: (44) (171) 937 8552.
Canada: *POINTERS,* 99 Yorkville Ave., Unit 103, Toronto,
Ontario M5R 3K5. Tel: (416) 962-9998 or (800) 465-5290,
Fax: (416) 962-6889.
Australia: *TAPESTRY ROSE,* PO Box 366, Canterbury Victoria
3126. Tel: (011) (61) 3 9804 0606.
New Zealand: *QUALITY HANDCRAFTS,* PO Box 1486,
Auckland. Tel: (64) (9) 411 8645, Fax: (64) (9) 307 1766.
South Africa: *SPEAKERS INTERNATIONAL,* Box 92043,
Norwood 2117. Tel: (27) 11 640 6722.

DECORATOR FABRICS:

DESIGNERS GUILD,
Osborne & Little, Inc.,
979 Third Ave., Ste. 520,
New York, NY 10022, U.S.A.
Tel: (212) 751-3333.

YARNS:

WESTMINSTER FIBERS,
5 Northern Boulevard,
Amherst, NH 03031, U.S.A.
Tel: (603) 886-5041.
Fax: (603) 886-1056
ROWAN, Green Lane Mill,
Washpit, Holmfirth,
Huddersfield HD7 1RW,
West Yorkshire, U.K.
Tel: (01484) 681 881.
Fax: (01484) 687 920.

PHOTO CREDITS:

CRAIG ANDERSON PHOTOGRAPHY: All photos in Chapter 5.
Flat shots on pages 87, 91, 95, 99, and 102–103.
DEBBIE PATTERSON: All other photography.
The inset shots on pages 10–13, courtesy of Random House UK, were
previously published in Kaffe Fassett's *Glorious Patchwork*
and *Glorious Interiors.*

Selected Books from Martingale & Company

CRAFTS

15 Beads: A Guide to Creating One-of-a-Kind Beads •
  Jane Dunnewold
The Art of Handmade Paper and Collage •
  Cheryl Stevenson
Fabric Mosaics • Terrece Beesley & Trice Boerens
Folded Fabric Fun • Nancy J. Martin
Grow Your Own Paper • Maureen Richardson
*Making Memories with Fabric, Photos, and Family
  Keepsakes* • Margaret Sindelar
Stamp with Style • Kathryn Perkins

HOME DECORATING

Decorate with Quilts & Collections • Nancy J. Martin
The Home Decorator's Stamping Book • Linda Barker
Living with Little Quilts • Alice Berg,
  Mary Ellen Von Holt & Sylvia Johnson
Make Room for Quilts • Nancy J. Martin
Soft Furnishings for Your Home • Sharyn Skrabanich
Special Occasion Table Runners • Janet Carija Brandt
Stitch & Stencil • Tessa Brown & Sheila Coulson
Welcome Home™: Debbie Mumm

BASIC QUILTMAKING TECHNIQUES

Basic Quiltmaking Techniques for Borders and Bindings •
  Mimi Dietrich
Basic Quiltmaking Techniques for Curved Piecing •
  Paulette Peters
Basic Quiltmaking Techniques for Divided Circles •
  Sherry Reis
Basic Quiltmaking Techniques for Eight-Pointed Stars •
  Sherry Reis
Basic Quiltmaking Techniques for Hand Appliqué •
  Mimi Dietrich
Basic Quiltmaking Techniques for Machine Appliqué •
  Maurine Noble
Basic Quiltmaking Techniques for Strip Piecing •
  Paulette Peters
Your First Quilt Book (or it should be!) • Carol Doak

NEEDLE ARTS

Baltimore Bouquets • Mimi Dietrich
Christmas Ribbonry • Camela Nitschke
Machine Needlelace and Other Embellishment Techniques •
  Judy Simmons
Miniature Baltimore Album Quilts • Jenifer Buechel
A Passion for Ribbonry • Camela Nitschke
A Silk-Ribbon Album • Jenifer Buechel
Simply Beautiful Sweaters: Tricoter • Beryl Hiatt &
  Linden Phelps
*Two Sticks and a String: Knitting Designs Inspired by
  Nature* • Kerry Ferguson
Victorian Elegance • Lezette Thomason

SURFACE DESIGN/FABRIC MANIPULATION

Complex Cloth • Jane Dunnewold
Creative Marbling on Fabric • Judy Simmons
Dyes and Paints • Elin Noble
Fantasy Fabrics • Bonnie Lyn McCaffery
Hand-Dyed Fabric Made Easy • Adriene Buffington
Jazz It Up • Judy Murrah

Many of these books are available at your
local fabric, quilt, or craft shop. Call, write,
fax, or e-mail for more information or to
request a free color catalog.

Martingale & Company
PO Box 118
Bothell, WA 98041-0118 USA

Toll-free: (800) 426-3126
Int'l: 425-483-3313
24-Hour Fax: 425-486-7596
E-mail: info@martingale-pub.com
Web: www.patchwork.com